"Do not let the br
Thornton has writte
book of Galatians. C
true exposition plain ... ...
new believer as well as the seasoned expositor."

Paul Washer, *founder and missions director of HeartCry Missionary Society*

"Many commentators today fall into one of two popular ditches when it comes to biblical commentaries. They either make the mistake of majoring on the side of practicality while ignoring doctrinal truth, or they major on doctrinal truth while ignoring practical matters at hand. One of the strengths of Chip Thornton is that he's fiercely committed to the original author's intent, which allows him to explain the doctrine faithfully within its proper context, while at the very same time providing helpful practical points from a pastoral perspective. We need more commentators like Chip Thornton who write in such a way to strengthen and encourage the church of Christ."

Josh Buice, *senior pastor of Pray's Mill Baptist Church in Douglasville, Georgia and president of G3 Ministries*

"While thorough exegetical commentaries are helpful and necessary, I have often longed for more pastoral commentaries that just get to the point. This is exactly what Chip Thornton has given us in the *Point-to-Point Biblical Commentaries* series. I am so thankful for his labors, and I am confident that this commentary will be quite useful to many pastors who desire to preach the text of Scripture."

Scott Aniol, *executive vice president and editor-in-chief of G3 Ministries and professor of pastoral theology at Grace Bible Theological Seminary*

"Chip Thornton serves pastors well by providing a readable, engaging, clear, and concise commentary on Galatians. Complete with sound exegesis, fresh illustrations, and striking applications, this resource offers a treasure trove of useful information. I will visit this volume every time I teach from this epistle."

Chris King, *senior pastor of Bayou View Baptist Church, Gulfport, Mississippi*

"This commentary offers readers the unique combination of conciseness, yet thorough exegesis. In this work Chip Thornton utilizes his own theological training and includes insights from some of the greatest theological minds, providing readers an expositional gold mine for preachers and students of Scripture. For any preacher seeking to preach through the book of Galatians, this is a necessary resource.

Kevin Blackwell, *assistant to the president for church relations and executive director of the Ministry Training Institute at Samford University*

CHIPLEY MCQUEEN THORNTON

Grace to You,

Chipley McQueen Thornton

GALATIANS

POINT-*to*-POINT
BIBLE COMMENTARIES

Press

Galatians: Justification by Faith
Point-to-Point Biblical Commentaries

Copyright © 2022 by Chipley McQueen Thornton

Published by G3 Press
4979 GA-5
Douglasville, GA 30135
www.G3Min.org

Printed in the United States of America by Graphic Response, Atlanta, GA

ISBN: 978-8-9855187-2-6

Cover Design: Joe Zarate

CONTENTS

INTRODUCTION

John Calvin famously wrote, "The chief excellency of an expounder consists in *lucid brevity*."[1] Commentators often quote this advice and try to follow it, but four hundred pages later, readers are left wondering what happened. I will try not to follow their example. I am more interested in Calvin's next sentence: "And, indeed, since it is almost his [the expositor's] only work to lay open the mind of the writer whom he undertakes to explain, the degree in which he leads away his readers from it, in that degree he goes astray from his purpose, and in a manner wanders from his own boundaries."[2] My task is simple: (1) to protect and preserve Paul's single meaning in each paragraph and (2) to do it with "lucid brevity." I will try. Many things will be left unsaid. I will try not to gloss over difficult verses. Forgive my brevity if I leave you unsatisfied.

---

[1] John Calvin, *Commentaries on the Epistle of Paul the Apostle to the Romans*, trans. John Owen (Edinburgh: Calvin Translation Society, 1849), xxiii, italics original.
[2] Calvin, *Romans*, xxiii.

Main Sources Consulted

(1) Martin Luther, *Commentary on Galatians*[3]
(2) John Calvin, *The Epistle to the Galatians*[4]
(3) Douglas Moo, *Galatians*[5]
(4) John MacArthur, *MacArthur Study Bible*[6]
(5) *ESV Study Bible.*[7]

Author

Galatians 1:1 identifies the Apostle Paul as the author. It was one of the first of his letters—if not the very first—which we have in Scripture.

Recipients

Paul writes to the **churches of Galatia (1:2)**. Galatia is in the vicinity of modern-day Turkey. Paul

---

[3] Martin Luther, *Commentary on the Epistle to the Galatians*, trans. Theodore Graebner (Grand Rapids: Zondervan, 1949). Available online at https://ccel.org/ccel/luther/galatians/.

[4] In John Calvin, *The Epistles of Paul the Apostle to the Galatians, Ephesians, Philippians and Colossians*, trans. T. H. L. Parker, Calvin's Commentaries (Grand Rapids: Eerdmans, 1965).

[5] Douglas J. Moo, *Galatians*, BECNT (Grand Rapids: Zondervan, 2013).

[6] John MacArthur, *The MacArthur Study Bible* (Nashville: Thomas Nelson, 1997).

[7] Wayne Grudem, ed., *The ESV Study Bible* (Wheaton, IL: Crossway, 2008).

planted churches in cities in southern Galatia on his first missionary journey (**Acts 13**). These congregations likely are his intended audience since he mentions he **preached the gospel to you at first** (**4:13**) (i.e., earlier). Paul probably wrote within a year of his first missionary journey.[8]

Situation

The first Christians struggled with serious questions we often take for granted:

1. Is a Jewish-Christian still required to follow the OT law? Must he still offer temple sacrifices (which were still in effect) to keep his salvation?
2. What about non-Jews (Gentiles)? They do not know the OT law. Must they conform to it? Must they be circumcised to be saved?

False teachers crept in to seize upon their confusion. They sought to undermine Paul and his gospel. For Paul, all such questions could be reduced to one: *How is a man made right (justified) with God?* His clear response: By faith in Christ, not our own works.

---

[8] Moo, *Galatians*, 76.

Purpose

MacArthur states the letter's purpose precisely: "Paul wrote Galatians to counter Judaizing false teachers who were undermining the central NT doctrine of justification by faith."[9]

Order of Salvation (*ordo salutis*)

Critical to understanding Galatians is Paul's *order of salvation*. Salvation is both a one-time event (justification) and a process (sanctification, perseverance). It began in eternity past with God's salvation plan. It continues in the present with the sinner's conversion and Christian walk. It ultimately finds completion at death when we receive our sinless, glorified bodies. Below is the classic (Pauline) *order of salvation*.

1.	Election	God's sovereign choice of a people for himself
2.	Gospel Call	The Holy Spirit's internal summons to conversion
3.	Regeneration	The Holy Spirit's resurrecting a dead soul to life
4.	Conversion	The sinner's repentance and faith in Christ's merits
5.	**Justification**	**God's declaration of right legal standing**

---

[9] MacArthur, *MacArthur Study Bible*, 1786.

6.	Adoption	God's formal acceptance of believers into his family
7.	Sanctification	The Holy Spirit's conforming believers into Christ's image
8.	Perseverance	The believer's ongoing obedience
9.	Death	The perishing of the mortal body
10.	Glorification	The receiving of the immortal body

Paul's chief concern in Galatians centers on #5: *justification* (explained below). This part of the salvation process was under attack. False teachers were making sanctification (#7) a prerequisite for justification (#5). Paul rightly discerned this rearrangement as a **different gospel** (**1:6**).

Contextual Points

Several points are important to keep in mind.

1. **Judaizers**. These are religious fanatics whom Paul characterizes in several ways:
    a. They **distort the gospel** (**1:7**)
    b. They claim a sinner is **justified before God by the law** (**3:11**)
    c. They demand observance of OT **days and months and seasons and years** for salvation (**4:10**)
    d. They teach that **circumcision** is required for salvation (**5:2–12**).

2. **Justification by Faith.** Paul considers the above requirements to be an assault on the gospel. The law's purpose is not to save us from sin, but to awaken us to our sin. Once awakened, the sinner must throw himself upon the mercies of Christ, who kept the law perfectly for us. Paul spells it out in these terms:
   a. The OT law cannot justify a sinner (**2:16**).
   b. Abraham was justified (by faith) *before* the law ever existed (**3:6**).
   c. The law's purpose was to *reveal* sin and *restrain* sin (**3:19–26**).
   d. God sent Jesus to fulfill the law for us (**4:4–5**).

To be justified by faith (Gal 2:16; 3:24), then, means:
   a. We have broken God's law.
   b. Jesus perfectly fulfilled the law(s) we broke.
   c. Jesus died and rose again to satisfy God's wrath for our law-breaking.
   d. The righteousness of Jesus is imputed to all who believe (**3:6**).

3. **Righteousness.** Imputed righteousness is the heart of justification by faith. To stand righteous before God, at least three things must occur: (1) the person must be free from "original" (or "inherited") sin; (2) the person must be free from "actual" transgressions; and, (3) the person must fulfill God's intent and design in the law. That is,

he/she must fulfill God's law perfectly, as Tyndale says, "from the ground of his heart:" meaning, with pure motives from the depths (or, "low bottom") of the heart-intentions.[10] This is impossible for human creatures born in sin. Therefore, we need the righteousness of Another. God freely offers to "credit" (impute) Christ's righteousness (his sinless nature and his sinless life) unto anyone who will accept it by faith. The sinner's faith is counted as righteousness. Theologians refer to this reckoning of righteousness as "imputed righteousness." The corollary doctrine to "imputed righteousness" is that God "credits" (imputes) their sins unto Christ, nailing their record of debt to the cross. Paul ferrets-out this "doctrine of imputation" in more detail in his subsequent letters (1 Cor 5:21; Rom 4:1-8; 5:12-21; Col 2:13-14), but it clearly stands as the driving force behind, this, his first letter. A person's sin-debt must be taken away. Then, he/she must declared righteous purely by faith in Christ. Abraham's experience, centuries before the law was even given, is a wonderful illustration of simple, saving faith: **Abraham "believed God and it was counted to him as righteousness" (3:6).**

---

[10] William Tyndale, "A Prologue to the Epistle of Paul to the Romans," in *Tyndale's New Testament* (New Haven: Yale University Press, 1989), 207. Tyndale was the first to translate the NT into English from the Greek manuscripts. His prologue, largely, translates Martin Luther's prologue to Romans.

4. **Negative View of Law?** Some believe Paul's sharply negative portrayal of the law in Galatians implies we should disassociate from the law altogether. Not so. Paul speaks positively of the law in Romans. In Galatians, he corrects abuses of the law.

Preaching Galatians

Preaching through Galatians is tricky. We can preach through it so slowly that we lose the thrust of the author's thought-flow. We can preach through it so quickly that we accomplish nothing more than a fly-through of its glorious truths. Calvin preached forty-three sermons from Galatians. As manly as that sounds, keep in mind that Calvin preached nearly every day (on alternate weeks). At this pace, it likely took him slightly over two months. For the modern pastor to preach forty-three sermons through Galatians would take about a year. This is probably too much. Today's listeners are more restless and distracted. What follows is a middle-ground approach that honors the thought-flow of Paul without getting bogged down in details not germane to his intention in this letter.

GALATIANS 1:1-9
HOW COULD YOU?

Paul writes to churches he planted in the region of Galatia. Members were struggling with this issue: Fanatics had crept in and asserted that members must keep the OT law to be saved. Paul greets the Galatians with a defense of his credentials, and then asks, "How could you turn away from the gospel I brought to you?"

Galatians 1:1-5. I Love You. Evident in Paul's greeting is a defense of his heavenly credentials. He accents an otherwise customary Greek greeting with several unique seedlings he later will develop: (1) the *origin* of his apostleship, (2) the *commission* of his apostleship, and (3) the *confirmation* of his apostleship. The *origin* of his apostleship is from **God the Father**, not **man**. The fanatics could not claim that. The *commission* of his apostleship was **through** the risen **Jesus Christ**. In **Acts 9:15,** Jesus told Ananias: **Go, for he [Paul] is a chosen instrument of mine to carry my name before the Gentiles and kings and the children of Israel**. This commission was spoken by the One who had been **raised from the dead**. The fanatics could not claim that either.

The *confirmation* of his apostleship was attested by **all the brothers who are with me**. That is, Paul's letter is affirmed by a wider Christian audience. Who are these brothers? We don't know. Yet, his impression is strong: Can the fanatics claim a wider Christian audience? Paul's emphasis is clear: My message is God's message. Theirs is not.

He writes to **the churches of Galatia** that he founded about a year prior. He greets them with two words: **grace** and **peace**. The Apostle is saying, "May God's favor (grace) and quiet calm (peace) rest upon you." This grace and peace come from the **Lord Jesus Christ, who gave himself for our sins**. This is an important phrase. It thunders down like a sledgehammer to crack the foundation of the fanatics' theology: If Christ gave himself for our sins, then no more sacrifice is necessary. Paul could have ended the letter here and won the argument. But he went further. Christ died **to deliver us**. The term *deliver*—nowhere else used by Paul—means to rescue from dire circumstances. Christ rescued us from this **present evil age**: namely, the kingdom of the devil. Christ's atoning work originated in the perfect **will of our God and Father**. That is, God knew that no man could fulfill the law. It was **according to the will of our God**—his passion, his burning desire—that he sent his Son to **deliver** us from the law's slavery.

Finally, Paul comes to the chief design of the gospel: The glory of God. **Galatians 1:5: To whom be the glory forever and ever**. The gospel exists not primarily for our therapeutic self-aggrandizement or to lift our self-esteem. The gospel exists to glorify (not us and who we are, but) God and who he is. It started in his will and it cost him his Son. It is stunning how well-intentioned souls make the gospel emphasis about *man* and *his* glory rather than *God* and *his* glory. That is precisely where the fanatics in Galatia were aiming: glorifying man and his works rather than God and God's works. The Apostle rightly discerns the motive of the gospel as the glory of God. Paul's (fairly typical) greeting makes two subtle, yet vital, points: (1) his calling is a heavenly one and (2) salvation is *in* Christ and *for* God's glory.

Galatians 1:6–9. I'm Disappointed in You! Each of us likely has different ways of confronting sin. There are times when it is best to be casual and relaxed (over a meal, perhaps). This was not one of them. At this point in Paul's letters, we typically find words of encouragement or thanksgiving. Not here. The shift is stark: **I am astonished that you are so quickly deserting him who called you in the grace of Christ and are turning to a different gospel!** I am stunned! I couldn't believe my ears! The Apostle narrows his brow and says to his spiritual children, "Let's cut to the chase."

Moo captures it: "He cannot thank God for them when their spiritual status is so uncertain."[11] You are so quickly deserting God. *How could you?* The word *deserting* is important. It means to change allegiance. Some liken those described by it to "spiritual turncoats."[12] Calvin

---

[11] Moo, *Galatians*, 75.

[12] Timothy George, *Galatians*, NAC 30 (Nashville: Broadman & Holman, 1994), 91.

speaks of their defection as turning to an "imaginary Christ" which is no Christ at all.[13] We can almost feel the Apostle's angst when we recognize the verb is in the present tense. That is: You are in the *act* of deserting, but you haven't deserted yet! There's still time! Do not advance another step! We can fix this![14] It almost has the feel of a marriage which is on the rocks, yet still may be saved.

They are turning to a different gospel. Luther is right: "Heretics do not advertise their errors."[15] Paul's gospel is this: Christ plus anything else (baptism, works, circumcision, papal edicts, etc.) is a different gospel. These fanatics **distort** (pervert) the true gospel. Calvin says their teaching "darkens the clearness of the gospel by ancient shadows."[16] They lead people away from God, and if away from God, then straight to hell.

To crush any objection, the Apostle appeals to angels (**1:8**): **But even if we or an angel from heaven should preach to you a gospel contrary to the one preached to you, let him be accursed**. Of course, the notion that an angel would proclaim another gospel is preposterous. That is precisely Paul's point. Angels are the emissaries of God (see **3:19**). Angels will in no way contradict that which has already been promised. Should someone come as an angel from heaven with a different gospel … Reject him! He is accursed: excommunicated, to be avoided, damned!

---

[13] Calvin, *Galatians*, 29.
[14] Calvin, *Galatians*, 30.
[15] Luther, *Galatians*, 26.
[16] Calvin, *Galatians*, 19.

The Apostle proceeds **(1:9)**: **If anyone is preaching a gospel contrary to the one you received, let him be accursed**. He speaks here in terms stronger than any of his other letters. He presents perversion of the gospel as if it is the greatest crime ever invented, and it is. Calvin calls it an "enormous crime." "When the glory of justification is ascribed to another," he says, "the doctrine of the gospel is ruined."[17] To preach a contrary gospel is to commit a spiritual felony. It robs Almighty God of his glory and invests it in depraved men! A contrary gospel slings mud on the cross! It is tantamount to committing spiritual high treason! No wonder the Apostle reserves his strongest language for such wicked fanatics. Spiritually, they are corrupting those whom Paul considers his children in the faith. Jesus pronounces a figurative death penalty on such deceitful workmen: "**Whoever causes one of these little ones who believe in me to sin, it would be better for him to have a great millstone fastened around his neck and to be drowned in the depth of the sea**" (**Matt 18:6**). Such men *should* be damned. Moo captures the moment, "What the agitators are teaching is not an interesting and inconsequential option ... they are teaching something that will, literally, lead themselves to hell."[18] Paul puts all on guard: This is not freedom of expression or an interpretational difference or a quirky view. This is demonic.

---

[17] Calvin, *Galatians*, 31.
[18] Moo, *Galatians*, 80.

Galatians 1:10. I Care Enough to Offend You.
Galatians 1:10 functions as swing verse to close one
thought and transition to another. That is, he closes his
sharp rebuke (of **1:6-9**), and then launches into a fiery defense of his ministry (**1:11ff**, as the connecting conjunc-
tion "**for**" indicates).

The Apostle was undeterred by the motives of
man: **For am I now seeking the approval of man, or of
God (1:10)?** Some situations are so urgent that man's approval doesn't matter. For instance, I once saved someone's life. An attorney and I were crossing a city street.
He was on the phone, distracted. I saw a huge bus steam-
rolling toward him. I grabbed him and jerked him back.
He was offended initially, but I didn't care. I was not
seeking his approval. I cared for his physical life. Spiritually, Paul conveys the same sentiment. He appeals to the
"testimony of a good conscience."[19] He esteems the ser-
vice of Christ greater than the approval of man. He cares
for them enough to offend them.

Sermon Summary

The preaching text is **Galatians 1:1-9** (although
1:10 should be included). We must resist the urge to get
bogged down in the greeting. There are a lot of good
points that *could* be made, but it is still a greeting meant
to say, "I love you in the Lord." The meaty doctrines will
follow. Wait until then to dig into them. Two points in the

---

[19] Calvin, *Galatians*, 36.

greeting should be brought to light: (1) Paul's apostleship has been sanctioned by God and (2) **Jesus gave himself for our sins**. The latter sets the tone for the rest of the letter. That phrase should be given the most attention: If the **Lord Jesus Christ gave himself for our sins** ... then his work cannot be added to or improved upon. Again, brevity is best here. State it and move on; the Apostle will expound this principle in detail later. For now, give it the same amount of weight in the sermon as Paul does in the letter: a passing jab to set up the knockout blow.

The bulk of the sermon should center on **1:6–9: I Am Disappointed in You**. The shift in tone tells us that this is the emphasis. Paul means business. He considers them his spiritual children—he being their father in the faith—and they are being seduced by spiritual evildoers. It must be stopped. Critical terms to expound include **deserting** (present tense; they are not gone yet), **distort** (pervert), and **accursed** (excommunicated, damned). Paul doesn't specifically define the true **gospel** here, although he did set its foundation earlier (**the Lord Jesus Christ gave himself for our sins**). Establish the gospel Paul taught when he founded these churches (he assumes they know it already). Jesus Christ alone: Not Jesus *plus* ANYTHING. Not Jesus *plus* circumcision (Judaizers); not Jesus *plus* church tradition (Catholics); not Jesus *plus* communion (Catholics); not Jesus *plus* baptism (Catholics, church of Christ, etc.); not Jesus *plus* works (Mormons, Jehovah's Witnesses); etc. Any additions distort (pervert) the true gospel.

A brief closing comment should mention **Galatians 1:10: I Care Enough to Offend You**. Paul sees a

train about to collide with his children. He cares enough
to forcefully shove them off the tracks since they are un-
aware of the impending doom. We shouldn't be surprised
if someone leaves offended by the exclusivity of Paul's
gospel. The fanatics also were offended. No matter. When
you take away man's glory and rightly replace it with God
alone, the heathen will rage. Let them rage. We please
God, not **man**.

GALATIANS 1:11–2:14
COME, LET US REASON TOGETHER

Paul launches into a defense of his gospel through personal testimony:

(1) I was saved out of a law-keeping life (**1:11–17**).
(2) I went to **Arabia** and back to **Damascus**.
(3) After three years, I connected with the apostles in **Jerusalem**.
(4) I went on mission to **Syria** and **Cilicia**.
(5) After fourteen years, I reconnected with the apostles. In this reconnection, two significant events occur: (a) the fanatics tried to impose their will on me (demanding I circumcise Titus) and (b) the fanatics cunningly swayed even the Apostle Peter to **fear** them.

Paul's testimony serves a twofold purpose: (1) to slam the door on any objection by the fanatics that Paul lacks authority (he rebuked the apostles themselves); (2) to tell these church members, "Listen, I know you are confused. You may be wondering, 'Who am I to trust?' Here are some solid reasons you can trust me." It is a lengthy defense: nearly a quarter of the entire letter. Its sheer length tips us off to its importance and indicates it should stand as its own sermon.

Galatians 1:11–17. Keep It (The Gospel) Simple. The fanatics made things complex. Paul says, "The gospel is simple. Keep it simple." He was not taught the gospel. It came to him by revelation: **For I would have you know, brothers, that the gospel that was preached by me is not man's gospel. For I did not receive it from any man, nor was I taught it, but I received it through a revelation of Jesus Christ** (1:11–12). Paul launches into a personal testimony of how he received it. **Acts 9** details his conversion, and we have no reason to doubt the congregations were aware of it. Indeed, he says, "**You have heard of my former life of Judaism**." **Acts 9:1** informs us he had been **breathing threats and murder against the disciples of the Lord**. In those days, Paul was a rising star in Judaism, a prodigy advancing rapidly. To fully appreciate his candor, we must understand his "old" view of the law. The original design of the law (as Paul later details, **Gal 3:15ff**) was *never* to save us, but rather to show us our wretchedness. Our constant failures were meant to drive us to Christ for mercy. Over time, the Jews began to teach that a man was saved by trying his best to keep the law, fail though he will. By the time Paul is born into the world, works-based salvation was in full force: "If you want to earn God's favor, obey the law," they said. Jews developed 613 meticulous rules to monitor obedience: you can't fry an egg on the Sabbath—that constitutes work; you can't wink at a relative—it could lead to incest; you can't eat pork; you can't shave your beard; you can't round corners on haircuts; you can't sow different seeds in the same field; and on and on. It was a complex set of rules that would make the IRS tax code proud.

He admits he was fervent for the "old" way: **And I was advancing in Judaism beyond many of my own age among my people, so extremely zealous was I for the traditions of my fathers** (1:14). When **God was pleased to reveal his Son** (1:16) to Paul, everything changed. The term *reveal* is important. It is *apokalypsai*, from which we get the term "apocalypse." *BDAG* defines it as the "divine revelation of certain transcendant secrets."[20] What secrets did the Son reveal? Simple: The Son alone had perfectly fulfilled all 613 rules *and* had applied his work to Paul's soul. Jesus said, **"Do not think that I have come to abolish the law or the Prophets; I have not come to abolish them but to fulfill them"** (Matt 5:17). Fulfill them for whom? For anyone who believes. The good news of the gospel is not complex. It is simple: Jesus Christ fulfilled the law because we couldn't. No more meticulous rule-keeping! No more condemnation for eating bacon! Freedom in Christ's righteousness freely given to me! Simple! So simple, it's easy to stumble over. This became Paul's "new" understanding of the law: The law cannot *save*, but it can aid in *sanctifying* the saved.

---

[20] W. Arndt, F. W. Danker, W. Bauer, and F.W. Gingrich, *A Greek-English Lexicon of the New Testament and other Early Christian Literature*, 3rd ed. (Chicago: University of Chicago Press, 2000), 112. Henceforth, *BDAG*.

He proceeds: "Once awakened to my sinful condition and trusting in Christ's righteousness, I was dis-
patched to the Gentiles. They didn't even know the law!
Can you believe it! To suggest (as the fanatics do) that
Gentiles must revert to law-keeping when the Son has
kept the law for us? Laughable! Christ fulfilled the law for
the Gentiles, too!"

Paul is speaking in plain language: "You want to
talk about Judaism and circumcision and law-keeping?
Ah! I *was* the law-man! I *was* the enforcer of the law! I ad-
vanced far beyond where these fanatics currently stand!
I know their heresies far better than they do because I
lived them. And I was once as miserable as they are now!
Don't be duped by these imposters!" The gospel is simple:
**God sent forth His Son, born of woman, born under
the law, to redeem those who were under the law, so
that we might receive adoption as sons (Gal 4:4)**! It's
the KISS principle: Keep it simple, stupid!

The Apostle says he "**went away into Arabia**."
Nowhere else in the Bible are we told he went to Arabia.
We are not told why, either. Some think he went there for
personal reflection and study. Others suggest he went
there as a missionary.[21] Scholars aren't even certain
about the exact location of Arabia.[22] What we *do* know is

---

[21] See Chuck Bumgardner's helpful article, online:
https://cbumgardner.wordpress.com/2011/11/18/paul-in-ara. Accessed April 9, 2022.

[22] Moo, *Galatians*, suggests it is either "a fairly large area to
the northeast, east, and south of Israel, including portions of Transjor-
dania, south Syria, the Negev, and the northwest Arabian Peninsula"

this: (1) Paul is establishing that he did not get his gospel from man (he went to Arabia, not Jerusalem) and (2) the gospel revealed by the Son transformed his life (and can transform yours, too)!

Galatians 1:18–2:10. Test Every Spirit. The Apostle counsels them to test the fanatics. Oftentimes, good things (such as the law) challenge the best things (such as the **gospel**). This is how tricky demonic spirits can be: They use good things to challenge the best thing.

He mentions that he went up to **Jerusalem** to connect with **Cephas** (henceforth, Peter). Then, he went on mission to the **regions of Cyria and Silicia**. We can say with some measure of confidence that he planted congregations in those regions since the Jerusalem Council letter (later) is addressed to **Gentiles in Antioch and Syria and Cilicia (Acts 15:23)**. Paul's intention in these lines is to document that the apostles—specifically, Peter and James—affirmed his ministry.

Galatians 2:1–10 gives rise to a debate in the commentaries which is not germane to this letter. I will mention it briefly. Some believe that **Galatians 2:1–10** is describing the Jerusalem Council in **Acts 15**.[23] Some don't.[24] To be fair, the Jerusalem Council grappled with this same issue: Fanatics were teaching, "**Unless you are circumcised according to the custom of Moses, you cannot be**

(106), but he also suggests it could have been a political designation for the Nabatean Kingdom.

[23] Moo, MacArthur.
[24] Calvin, ESV, George in NAC.

saved" (**Acts 15:1**). The Jerusalem Council concluded it was best not to trouble the Gentiles with such rituals. However, in order for Christian Gentiles to maintain fellowship with Christian Jews, they proposed the Gentiles merely abstain from certain foods and from sexual immorality. I don't believe **Galatians 2:1–10** is referring to the Jerusalem Council for two reasons: (1) The Jerusalem Council gave Paul the ammunition he needed to destroy the fanatics once for all. He certainly would have unleashed it here if he'd had it in his arsenal. (2) Here in Galatians, Peter feared the fanatics on this very issue (**2:11–14**); there (**Acts 15:6–21**), Peter argued decidedly against them. Regardless, Paul's greater point is this: *Test every spirit against the gospel.*

A significant event occurs in this section: Justification by faith in Christ is directly challenged. Paul recognized this and would not **yield ... for a moment**. He was summoned to **Jerusalem** by divine **revelation**—not by the apostles—to **make sure he was not running in vain**. He wanted to make certain that he and the apostles were in unison rather than divided on the doctrine of justification by faith alone. The controversy reared its ugly head when the fanatics demanded that Paul's companion, Titus, be **circumcised**. Paul sees the demand for what it is: An attack on the gospel. He discerns the inner motive of these fanatics, calling them **false brothers (2:4)**. They demonically **slipped in to spy out our freedom ... so that they might bring us into slavery**. As mentioned above, he speaks of spiritual **slavery** under the law.

The Apostle acts heroically: **We did not yield in submission even for a moment**! Someone might object,

"What's this? Of all things to quibble over, Paul quibbles over circumcision? Why not make peace? Right or wrong, why cause Jewish brothers to stumble?" The Apostle, excellent defender of the gospel that he was, glares at them straight in the eye and responds unflinchingly, "Never! You cannot make peace with demons. More is at stake here than Christian harmony. The gospel is under siege! These are not 'weaker' brothers! These are false brothers! They were not invited in! They slipped in! They do not have pure motives! They spy! They lurk! They crouch, ready to pounce! No, this is not about Titus or circumcision. This is about power, control, and devilish doctrines designed to rip the heart from the gospel!"

Call him a lightning rod if you will: Paul dug his heels into the dirt, stood strong, and single-handedly withstood this gospel assault! Bravo to the Apostle! He saw clearly the future implications: **The truth of the gospel** was at stake! His valiant defense **preserved** the gospel **for you**. Herein lies the truth: If you add anything to the gospel, the gospel perishes! Stand with the Apostle and say, "It shall never be!"

He goes on to recount how the Jerusalem apostles accepted his full apostolic authority, specifically in regard to the **Gentiles (2:6–10)**. Yet, the thrust here is the all-out attack by these agitators on poor Titus. Circumcision is a good thing. It is biblical: as are holy days and baptism and Christian traditions and obedience to the law. These "good" things, however, must never rise-up to challenge the "best" thing. When it does, we must rise-up with the Apostle and protect the gospel. He tested their spirits in light of the pure gospel, and the light of the pure gospel exposed their dark spirits.

Galatians 2:11-14. Stand Your (Gospel) Ground. The fanatics had, cunningly, influenced even the Apostle Peter: **But when Cephas came to Antioch, I opposed him to his face, because he stood condemned (2:11)**. As excellent an apostle as Peter was, these spiritual monsters frightened him. Peter dined with Gentiles in Antioch, a "no-no" for devout Jews, but a perfectly acceptable activity for a Christian man. Undoubtedly, he enjoyed foods forbidden by the law, but—again—perfectly acceptable under the gospel. When the fanatics appeared (**the circumcision party**), Peter—**and the rest of the Jews** (even **Barnabas**) **drew back** and **separated** themselves from their Gentile brothers. How could this be? The Apostle Paul smelled hypocrisy. He sat back, rubbed his chin, and realized: Peter altered his behavior out of **fear** of **the circumcision party (2:12)**. What Christian acts this way? How are the Gentile Christians to feel when you show such discrimination? The Apostle exposed Peter's hypocrisy (as well as that of the others) in the presence of all: **If you, though a Jew, live like a Gentile and not like a Jew, how can you force the Gentiles to live like Jews (2:14)?** Peter's problem was the fanatics had some leverage over him: be it political, financial, emotional, or otherwise (though he later realized the error of his ways and stood strong at the Jerusalem Council). What we know with certainty is this: **Their conduct was not in step with the truth of the gospel (2:14)**. They did not have the clear conscience of Paul. They were more interested in pleasing man than God (**1:10**). This must never be. We admit: Every hill is not a hill on which to die. But this one was. Fear of man must never excuse us from standing our gospel ground. It takes guts to stand against close friends or relatives (Barnabas), associates (Peter and the rest of the Jews), and evil groups (such as the circumcision party). But we always must be prepared to answer these two questions: (1) Is this a hill on which to die? (2) Am I seeking the approval of man, or of God?

Sermon Summary

This preaching text is **Galatians 1:11–2:14**. It divides itself neatly into three sections. The first deals with the Paul's conversion from the "old" understanding the law to the simplicity of trusting Christ as our law-keeper. The second section recounts several events, the most important being Paul's defense of the gospel against those perverting it. The third demonstrates how Paul single-handedly defended God's gospel. I would title the sermon something like, "**You've Got to Stand for Something or You'll Fall for Anything.**" Briefly mention **Galatians 1:10** (a swing verse) to transition into this preaching text. The following points capture the thrust of Paul's message:

I.   **Keep It (The Gospel) Simple (1:11–17)**

II.   **Test Every Spirit (Against the Gospel) (1:18–2:10)**

III. **Stand Your (Gospel) Ground (2:11–14)**

GALATIANS 2:15-21
LISTEN, AGAIN,
TO THE GOSPEL I TAUGHT YOU

In a tightly woven argument, Paul seizes on Peter's hypocrisy to show its implications for the doctrine of justification by faith. He anticipates his opponents' objection: "Discarding the law for salvation—as Paul suggests—makes us no different than the Gentiles. Worse, it turns Christ into a promoter of their sin!" Paul answers emphatically (if not angrily), "**Certainly not!**" It's as if he cries, "Preposterous! You have the wrong view of justification entirely!" For Paul, salvation is both a one-time event (i.e., *regeneration, conversion, justification* and *adoption* happen simultaneously) and an ongoing process (i.e., *sanctification* and *perseverance* happen over time). Remember, Paul's *order of salvation* is:

11.	Election	God's sovereign choice of a people for Himself (Eph 1:4-6)
12.	Gospel Call	The Holy Spirit's internal summons to Conversion (Rom 10:13)
13.	Regeneration	The Holy Spirit's resurrecting a dead soul to life (Eph 2:5)

14.	Conversion	The sinner's repentance and faith in Christ's merits (Eph 1:13)
15.	**Justification**	**God's declaration of right legal Standing (Rom 4:23–25)**
16.	Adoption	God's formal acceptance of believers into his family (Eph 1:5)
17.	Sanctification	The Holy Spirit's conforming believers into Christ's image (Rom 6:19)
18.	Perseverance	The believer's ongoing obedience (Rom 5:3–4)
19.	Death	The perishing of the mortal body (1 Cor 15:21)
20.	Glorification	The receiving of the immortal body (1 Cor 15:42)

Paul rightly recognized that the fanatics had disrupted this order. In doing so, they had created a false gospel. They asserted sanctification was necessary before God would justify the sinner, an unthinkable notion! The Apostle saw through that subtle, but heretical, twist. Doctrinal precision matters. The fanatics cleverly had flipped the gospel on its head. "The law cannot save (**2:16**), it can only condemn!" cries the Apostle. Peter, for instance, was **not in step with the truth of the gospel (2:14**): He reverted back to law-keeping when he refused to eat with Gentiles (although we should be kind to Peter: He later found his gospel grit and heroically defended the gospel of grace at the Jerusalem Council). To Paul, Peter's act of hypocrisy screamed out, "**Christ died for no purpose!**" (**2:21**). His point is clear: To add any works of the law to Christ's works (by refusing to eat with Gentiles, for example) slings mud on the cross!

Galatians 2:15-16. Let Me Be Clear. Paul plainly lays down the doctrine of justification: **by the works of the law no one will be justified (3:16)**. Jews, when compared with Gentiles, *seem* pretty good: Jews have the law, the ordinances, the oracles of God, the promises, etc. Paul concludes, "**We ourselves are Jews by birth and not Gentile sinners**" (2:15). "**Yet** ..." (**2:16**). Paul shifts gears. Their Jewish experience proved they could not keep the law God gave them. They violated it daily. This alone should convince them it can't save: "You're missing the purpose of the law altogether!" reasons the Apostle, "The design of the law is not to save. The design of the law is to condemn, to awaken us to our sinful condition (*regeneration*) ... so that we will call upon the name of the Lord to save us from the law that continually slays us (*conversion*)!" Then, and only then, will God declare sinners righteous by applying Christ's merits to them (*justification*). Now, man's view of the law changes entirely. Whereas once it was hideous (constantly slaying sinners), it now becomes beautiful (guiding believers in godliness).

Galatians 2:17. Here Is Their Objection. The fanatics object, "If you have received Christ's righteousness, why do you still sin? Now, Paul, you have turned Christ into a **servant of sin**!" What did they mean by asserting Christ was a "**servant of sin**?" Calvin explains:

He puts a question, in his usual manner, into the mouth of his antagonists. "If, in consequence of the righteousness of faith, we, who are Jews and were 'sanctified from the womb' (Jer. i.5; Gal. i.15), are reckoned guilty and polluted, shall we say that Christ makes sin to be powerful in his own people, and that he is therefore the author of sin?"[25]

The answer to Calvin's question, of course, is a resounding, "No." But you see the agitators' implication. Moo brings it into perspective, "Pauls asks if Christ, in . . . requiring Jewish Christians to abandon their allegiance to torah [i.e., the law] as the authoritative revelation of their conduct, is 'serving' or 'leading others to commit' sin."[26]

Galatians 2:18. Christ Set You Free. Paul responds: If I sin, it is me that sins—not Christ in me. He offers a simple illustration. **For if I rebuild what I tore down, I prove myself to be a transgressor.** That is, Jesus Christ tore down the wall (the law) dividing Jew and Gentile. If I go about **rebuilding** the law that Christ **tore down**, then I'm the **transgressor**. In this case, Peter was **rebuilding** the law by his hypocrisy. Peter was the **transgressor**, not Christ!

---

[25] Calvin, *Galatians*, 71.
[26] Moo, *Galatians*, 165.

Galatians 2:19-20. Justification Results in Transformation. Here Paul speaks of the *result* of justification, a transformed life: **For through the law I died to the law, so that I might live to God (2:19)**. The phrase, "**through the law**" might be confusing. Calvin helpfully explains, "But it is the law which forces us to die to itself; for it threatens our destruction, leaves us nothing but despair, and thus drives us away from trusting to the law."[27] In other words, the thunder of the law awakens sinners to their sinful condition. Once justified, the sinner lives to God, not the law. Theologians call this *sanctification*. Others call it the "Christian walk." Once a sinner is declared righteous, his life will begin to transform. Over time, he will sin less and hate sin more. Paul explains: **I died to the law**. What exactly does this phrase mean? It means the law holds no power over him to condemn. Recently, a famous athlete died in prison while on trial for murder. Once dead, the law no longer had no power over him. Paul died to the law—spiritually—so the law no longer controlled him. Christ did. Tyndale rightly remarked, "The fruit maketh not the tree good, but the tree the fruit."[28]

The fanatics claimed, "You must live to the law or be dead to God." Paul waves a finger in the air: "No, no!" says he, "You must die to the law to live to God." Then he says, **I have been crucified with Christ (2:20)**. Christ's crucifixion was meant to satisfy the wrath of God for

---

[27] Calvin, *Galatians*, 72.
[28] William Tyndale, *The Parable of the Wicked Mammon*, 1527 (accessible online).

every law-breaker who would believe by faith. To be crucified with Christ is to be freed from the "curse and guilt
of the law"[29] as well as its penalty: eternal damnation.

The next critical phrase is: **It is no longer I who
live, but Christ lives in me** (2:20). Here Paul speaks of
the "Spirit of Christ," living in him (the Holy Spirit). His
meaning: "I stand justified before God by faith. The law
now has no control over me. God freely gifts me with a
love-gift: Christ's Spirit. This union with Christ, inside
me, transforms me to greater levels of sanctification than
the law could ever produce! No longer is it my duty to
keep the law! It is my delight! Oh, glorious day! I **live in
the flesh** and desire fleshly things, but Christ's Spirit
domiciles in me, too! He continually sanctifies me,
teaches me, convicts me, reforms me, molds me into his
image! I am by no means perfect. But his Spirit is progres-
sively transforming me from the inside out: something
the old law could never do." God's justification sends into
the sinner the Spirit of Christ. The Apostle can say now,
**The life I now live in the flesh I live by faith in the Son
of God** (2:20).

Motive is critical. The motive of the fanatics was
law-keeping to *earn* salvation. The motive of Paul was
law-keeping as the *fruit* of salvation. Luther quips, "The
tree makes the apple; the apple does not make the tree."
Justification produces fruit. Fruit cannot produce justification.

---

[29] Calvin, *Galatians*, 74.

Galatians 2:21. Don't Sling Mud on the Cross. God provided all righteousness for you. If you seek to add it, then you are saying **Christ died for no purpose**. It would be like saying to God, "Your Son's life and brutal death and glorious resurrection was not good enough. I must add to it to make it perfect." That is tantamount to slinging mud on the cross.

Sermon Summary

The preaching text is **Galatians 2:15-21**. This will be a doctrinal sermon. The outline is simple. Follow Paul's thought-flow:

(1) State the doctrine.   **Let Me Be Clear (2:15-16)**

(2) State the objection.   **Here Is Their Objection (2:17)**

(3) State the response.   **Christ Set You Free (2:18)**

(4) State the application.   **Justification Results in Transformation (2:19-20)**

(5) State the conclusion.   **Don't Sling Mud on the Cross (2:21)**

One connection to make is this: Paul launches into this doctrine after seizing on Peter's hypocrisy. It will be important to show how Peter's actions threatened the doctrine of justification by faith alone.

GALATIANS 3:1-14
LET'S COMPARE LAW AND GOSPEL

Here the Apostle begins to systematically dismantle the fanatics' argument. He starts by asking rhetorical questions that seem ridiculous but which skillfully carve-up their false gospel (**3:1-5**). Next, he shows them the **gospel** in the OT. Several points are helpful to know from the outset:

(1) What does **foolish** mean (**3:1**)? Paul uses the term in two other places to describe lost people (**Tit 3:3**) and those who fall prey to materialism (**1 Tim 6:9**). Here, it is a rebuke of the Galatians for failure to see the obvious.

(2) What does **bewitched** mean (**3:1**)? It means to "exert evil influence through the eye."[30] These wicked false teachers have introduced an evil spiritual influence.

(3) What does **publicly portrayed** mean (**3:1**)? Paul likely is referring to vivid word pictures he used when he originally preached to them.

---

[30] Moo, *Galatians*, 181.

(4) What does **suffer** mean (**3:4**)? **Galatians 4:29** indicates some may have been persecuted. Paul had warned them from the outset: **through many tribulations we must enter the kingdom of God (Acts 14:22)**.

Galatians 3:1-6. Can the Law Do This? After defending, Paul counterattacks. He rebukes the Galatians for being duped by these spiritual snake-oil salesmen: **O foolish Galatians! Who has bewitched you (3:1)?** He asks three questions that frame the matter handily:

(1) Did the law give you the Holy Spirit (**3:2**)?
(2) Did the law make you perfect (**3:3**)?
(3) Did the law save Abraham (**3:6**)?

Then why are you so **foolish** to believe the law has saving power? **Galatians 3:6** is another swing verse. It closes this section and transitions into his next point by recalling Abraham.

Galatians 3:7-14. Let Me Show You from Your OT. The key to understanding Paul's use of the OT is the word *rely* in **Galatians 3:10: For all who rely on the works of the law are under a curse**. The fanatics were "relying" on the law to justify them. It cannot. The OT texts Paul cites never teach that the law justifies. Rather, the law is the guide to godly living (after justification). The law, for the God-fearer, becomes the guide to enjoying life under God's pleasure. Violating it invites God's discipline, but never alters his declaration of righteousness. The commentaries spend countless pages pondering whether Paul cited the OT verses out of context. Nonsense! He was making a point: If you **rely** on the law for justification, then you live under its **curse**. If you **rely** on the law to get you to heaven, then you will be subject to the law's penalty each time you break it. "Don't **rely** on the law to justify," the Apostle cries, "It has no power to do so." Rather, Christ redeemed us from the curse of the law . . . **so that in Christ Jesus the blessing of Abraham might come (3:14)**.

Paul demonstrates this from the OT. He lifts Abraham as the prime example. Then, he rattles off a litany of supporting verses from the OT. His point is that these fanatics are under a curse for "relying" on the law.

Genesis 15:6: Abraham Justified by Faith. Paul states, **Abraham believed God, and it was counted to him as righteousness**. His point? Abraham did nothing to earn justification. He believed God's promises. God imputed righteousness to Abraham based on his simple faith.

Genesis 12:3: The Gospel Was Preached to Abraham. Paul calls **Genesis 12:3** to bear witness in **Galatians 3:9**. God promised Abraham: **In you shall all nations be blessed**. In that phrase, we find the gospel in seedling-form. Scripture foresaw three ways that gospel seedling would sprout: (1) Abraham would become Israel. (2) Christ would come out of Israel. (3) All nations would be blessed by hearing Christ's gospel.

Hindsight informs Paul: **The Scripture, foresee-
ing that God would justify the Gentiles by
faith, preached the gospel beforehand to
Abraham, saying, "In you shall all nations be
blessed."**

**Deuteronomy 27:26: If You Break One Law,
You Are Guilty.** Here is the nut of it: **For all who
rely on works of the law are under a curse, for
it is written, "Cursed be everyone who does
not abide by all things written in the Book of
the Law, and do them"** (3:10). The context of
this Deuteronomy text is Moses giving God's people the law. He called Israel together and pro-
nounced blessings for following the law and
curses for breaking it. Moses ends by saying,
**"Cursed be anyone who does not confirm the
words of this law by doing them"** (Deut 27:26).
Moses's people were not "relying" on the law for
justification. The law was their guide to manifold
blessings and sanctification. The Galatians, on
the other hand, were being taught to **rely** upon
the law for justification. Those who **rely** on the
law for justification are under its **curse**. All Jews
knew from experience that they break the law re-
peatedly. What's more, the penalty for breaking
one law is the same as the penalty for breaking
them all. Therefore, Paul reasons in **3:11: Now it
is evident that no one is justified before God
by the law**.

Habakkuk 2:4: Habakkuk Said This Long Ago.
Next, Paul tells them, "Go read Habakkuk." Centuries ago, the prophet proclaimed, **The righteous shall live by faith (3:11)**. Habakkuk made
this pronouncement when Babylon was march-
ing to destroy Jerusalem and take God's people
captive. In anticipation of impending doom, Habakkuk recognized the law could not save them. A
person's only hope was to live by faith that God
would accomplish his plan. Paul uses this verse
similarly: The law cannot save you from spiritual
destruction. Rather, **the righteous shall live by
faith** that God would save them "in Christ."

**Leviticus 18:5: If You Rely on the Law, You
Will Be Judged by It**. The Apostle presses on: **But
the law is not of faith, rather, "The one who
does them shall live by them" (3:12)**. Moses
originally wrote this verse in his preface to sexual
purity laws. That is, **if a person does them** [i.e.,
follows them], **he shall live by them** [i.e., enjoy
God's blessings]. However, if a man is "relying"
on those laws for salvation, then he will be judged
by the very laws on which he "relies."

**Deuteronomy 21:23: Christ Became Your
Curse**. Paul remembered Moses's words, **Cursed
is everyone who is hanged on a tree (3:13)**. Moses wrote that a perpetrator hanged on a tree is
cursed by God. Paul's point is that all have broken the law and deserve to be hanged on a tree.

But Christ **redeemed** us by hanging on a tree in our place. He became our curse.

Finally, the Apostle finishes-out the doctrine of imputed righteousness. Christ **redeemed** us *not only* by taking on our death penalty. In return, he gave us the **blessing of Abraham**, which is Christ's imputed righteousness. Along with that imputed righteousness comes God's down payment: **the promised Spirit (3:14)**.

Sermon Summary

Paul compares the law with the gospel to show the Galatians how they had been deceived. The sermon points fall into two distinct sections: (1) sarcastic questions that make a serious point and (2) OT attestation of his point. I outlined the text something like this:

Title: Let's Compare the Law and the Gospel

I.   **Can the Law Do This? (3:1-6)**
        A. Give the Spirit? (3:1-2)
        B. Make You Perfect? (3:3-4)
        C. Save Abraham? (3:5-6)
II.   **Listen to the OT (3:7-14)**
        **A. If You Break One Law, You Are Guilty
            of All (3:7-10)**
        **B. Habakkuk Spoke This Long before Me
            (3:11)**

    C. If You Rely on the Law, You Will Be Judged by It (3:12)

    D. God Imputed Our Death-Curse to Christ (3:13)

    E. God Imputed Christ's Blessing to Us (3:14)

The temptation is to get bogged down in the multiple OT texts cited. Paul didn't. Therefore, the sermon shouldn't. His purpose in stringing them together is tied-back to the word *rely* in **3:10**. The OT saints were not **relying** on the law for salvation. The fanatics were. Accordingly, they were under its **curse** rather than its **blessing**. The OT saints were resting by faith in God's promise. So should we.

GALATIANS 3:15–4:7
WHAT IS THE RELATIONSHIP
BETWEEN LAW AND GOSPEL?

The Apostle explains the relationship between the law and the gospel. He does so in an organized fashion: (1) a human example (**3:15–18**); (2) a couple of clarifying questions (**3:19–20**); (3) a concluding thought (**3:27–29**); and (4) an application (**4:1–7**).

Galatians 3:15–18. A Promise Is a Promise. A promise is a promise, says the Apostle. Martin Luther summarized it succinctly: "The Law was never meant to cancel the promise.... The Law was meant to confirm the promise."[31] God is not so fickle as to make a promise and then change it. The Apostle likens it to a last will and testament. Generally speaking, once **ratified**, it becomes irrevocable.

The Apostle gets lawyerly at this point. He makes a linguistic point in **v. 16**: **Now the promises were made to Abraham and to his offspring. It does not say, "And to offsprings," referring to many, but referring to**

---

[31] Luther, *Galatians*, 121.

one, **"And to your offspring," who is Christ**. Paul is making what we call an "exegetical" argument. He's likely referring to the first time God speaks of offspring to Abraham, **Genesis 13:14–15: The LORD said to Abram, after Lot had separated from him, "Lift up your eyes and look from the place where you are, northward and southward and eastward and westward, for all the land that you see I will give to you and to your offspring forever."** The Apostle argues that since *offspring* is singular here, it is referring to a singular individual, Christ. At the same time, Paul is not so obtuse as to demand that offspring always refer to an individual. In **Galatians 3:29**, we see that he himself uses offspring as a plural; namely, that we (believers) are the spiritual offspring of Abraham. Taken in context, though, the Apostle sees Jesus Christ as *the* offspring (singular) who begets spiritual offspring (plural).

Remember, Paul was a lawyer and loved this kind of complex exegesis. The point he makes, though, is simple enough: God made a promise to Abraham and to Christ, his offspring (singular). It stands irrevocable. God made this promise 430 years before the law was given. The law, then, could never justify Abraham, nor can it justify any man. Luther offers a useful anecdote:

> A man of great wealth adopts a strange boy as his son.... In due time he appoints the boy as heir to his entire fortune. Several years later the old man asks the boy to do something for him. And the young boy does it. Can the boy then go around

and say that he deserved the inheritance by his obedience to the old man's request?[32]

Galatians 3:19–26. What Then Is the Law's Purpose? Paul asks the natural question, **Why then the law (3:19)?** Answer: The law serves a two-fold purpose: (1) to restrain sin and (2) to reveal sin. First, the law *restrains* sin: **It was added because of transgressions, until the offspring should come to whom the promise had been made (3:19).** This is its "civil" purpose. The law restrains the wicked hearts of men. If no law existed, the rage and terror of men would be ever so great. We might think society is bad today. Imagine how much worse it would be with no law to restrain sin. Second, the law *reveals* sin: **But the Scripture imprisoned everything under sin, so that the promise by faith in Jesus Christ might be given to those who believe (3:22).** This is its "spiritual" purpose. The Scripture, at the time the Apostle wrote, was the OT law. He continues, **we were held captive under the law (3:23).** That is, the law exposes our iniquities, makes us aware of our sinful condition, and confronts us with our utter wretchedness. Without the law, we would be blind to our savage, self-righteous nature. Luther says, "God must therefore first take the sledgehammer of the Law in His fists and smash the beast of self-righteousness.... When the conscience has been thoroughly frightened by the Law, it welcomes the Gospel of grace."[33] The law must wound before the gospel can

---

[32] Luther, *Galatians*, 122.
[33] Luther, *Galatians*, 129.

heal. The law is a spiritual mirror that shines light on the errors of our ways. It exposes our hidden flaws. But it cannot save. All it can do is reveal. In fact, it **imprisoned** us under its heavy-handed warden (**3:23**).

The Apostle refers to the law as our guardian: **But now that faith has come, we are no longer under a guardian (3:24)**. A first-century guardian was a slave assigned to monitor the behavior of young children.[34] Often, the guardian would use force to regulate the child's behavior. We were imprisoned under the supervision of the law-warden until **Christ came (3:24)**. Christ set us free from the law-warden's oppressive regime. Christ alone fulfilled every intent and design of the law and gifted that perfection to us. When we **put on Christ (3:26)**, we put on his letter-perfect law-keeping life as our own. In summary, the law has a dual function: (1) a *civil* function to keep men's transgressions in check and (2) a *spiritual* function to magnify spiritual imperfections. Both work together to drive us to despair so that our only hope is to cry out, "I am a wretch! I need the righteousness of Another!"

Galatians 3:27–29. Justification by Faith Levels the Playing Field. Justification is non-discriminatory: **There is neither Jew nor Greek ... slave nor free ... male nor female, for you are all one in Christ Jesus**. You needn't be smart to be justified. You needn't be Jewish. You needn't be esteemed of men. You needn't be educated. You needn't be a male. You needn't be an adult.

---

[34] Moo, *Galatians*, 243.

At the most basic level, all humans have one thing in common: Sin. And all humans are saved by one thing: Faith. All who trust in Christ by faith are equally righteous because each receives the full measure of Christ's righteousness: **heirs according to promise (3:29)**. We receive the same inheritance as heirs.

Galatians 4:1–7. Let Me Tell You What Your Father Did. An illustration: **The heir, as long as he is a child, is no different from a slave, though he is owner of everything, but is under guardians or managers until the date set by his father (4:1–2)**. As adults, we often find out that good fathers did many things for us that, in childhood, we were not privy to. For instance, consider the father who put much money into a trust to be distributed to his son on his 18th birthday. The father had the child attend military school throughout his formative years. On his 18th birthday, he graduated from the school (that held him captive, so to speak), and he received the full benefit of the trust fund. The son had no idea while he was in military school what financial blessings were in store. Paul tells a similar story. Take a slavemaster's son. In one sense, the son owns nothing. Yet, in another sense, he owns everything. He is raised by the master's slaves. He plays with the slave boys. His guardian is a slave. He is **no different** from a slave ... **until the date set by his father**. Then, the slave that had been over him suddenly becomes a worker for his benefit. The same is true spiritually. We were slaves to the law. But on the date set by the Father, the law that had been over us suddenly became a guide for our benefit.

Paul leaves this illustration for a discussion of the steps the Father took to secure that switcharoo: **But when the fullness of time had come, God sent forth his Son, born of woman, born under the law, to redeem those who were under the law, so that we might receive adoption as sons** (4:4–5). Ah! The gospel! When the time was ripe (in the fullness of time), God sent forth his Son. Jesus was born under the law. He came to redeem, an important term that reminds us of slaves on a trading block. While we were slaves to the law, Christ came to **redeem** us from the law's shackles. Then, God adopted us (**4:5**). Not only so, God gave us a gift: He **sent the Spirit of his Son into our hearts, crying, "Abba! Father!"** (4:6). His Spirit lovingly guides us whereas the law had unforgivingly assailed us. Think of it: God was working on your behalf when you weren't aware of it: (1) he sent his Son (**4:4**); (2) his Son perfectly fulfilled the law (**4:5**); (3) his Son redeemed us from the law's grip (**4:5**); (4) God adopted us as sons (**4:6**); (5) God gifted us with his Spirit (**4:6**); and, (6) God made us heirs with all the rights and privileges of his kingdom bestowed upon us (**4:7**). All of this was unbeknownst to us. Even our turning to him and crying out—Abba! Father!—is a work of his grace in us by sending Christ's Spirit into our hearts! Amazing!

Sermon Summary

The thought-flow of this section runs from **3:15–4:7**. I was tempted to take **4:1–7** as its own sermon because it is such a concise picture of how God saves sinners. However, if you remove the chapter divisions, **4:1–7** belongs in this sermon. In this section, Paul invites the Galatians to **Think It Through** from several angles: (1) God's nature (he keeps his promises) (**3:15–18**); (2) the law complements rather than contradicts the gospel (**3:19–29**); (3) the gospel has relevance in the here-and-now (**4:1–7**). The temptation for preachers/teachers is to get tied up in endless musings on **offspring** versus **offsprings** (**3:16**) or **angels** and **intermediaries** (**3:19–20**) when the point the Apostle makes in each paragraph is elementary:

I.   **A Promise Is a Promise (3:15–18)**
II.   **The Law Has a Two-fold Purpose (3:19–26)**
III. **Rely on What God Did for You, not What You Do for God (4:1–7)**

A good title might be: **Think It Through.** Point 1 establishes that the promise came 430 years before the law, and God doesn't break his promises. Point 2 shares God's purpose in giving the law: (a) to restrain sin and (2) to reveal sin. Point 3 enlightens us as to how God was working in the background for our benefit without us even realizing it.

GALATIANS 4:8–20
WE NEED TO TALK

The theme which dominates this section is heart-sickness. Look at the terms Paul uses: **afraid** for them (**4:11**), in **anguish** (**4:19**), **perplexed** (**4:20**). It reads as if one person (the Galatian church) abandoned a long-term relationship (with God) for a previously abusive lover (the law). The parent (Paul) is spilling his guts trying to awaken his children to their senses. Perhaps you have written such a letter. Before writing it, you pore over matters in your heart. The letter itself is the overflow of serious thought, prayers, and emotion. Paul is no different.

Galatians 4:8–11. Here's What You *Need* to Hear (Not What You *Want* to Hear). In nearly every relationship, there is a "come to Jesus" moment. This is it. After laying out the doctrine of justification beautifully, the Apostle leans in to speak, emotionally, to their hearts. "I don't get it," he seems to say, "You want to go back to your old lover (the things that **enslaved you**)?" They had **come to know** someone who treated them much better: **God**. Better yet, he stooped down to know them. It's almost as if the Apostle is asking, "You want to go back to your abusive relationship, where the law is beating you all the time?" Why go back to such a **weak** and **worthless** existence? The phrase **you were enslaved** (**4:8**) probably refers to the law (for Jews) or the idols (for Gentiles). Both can enslave. He mentions they had returned to observing the tedious **days and months and season and years** (**4:10**) the OT prescribed, which were shadows of Christ's coming. Then ... he finally states it outright: **I am afraid I may have labored over you in vain** (**4:11**). "There! You want me to say it?" the Apostle cries. "There! I am afraid you aren't saved." That is a tough conversation to have, but many today need to have that tough conversation.

Galatians 4:12–16. What Changed? The Apostle had held in his true feelings long enough: "I'm not certain you're truly saved." Now, he circles back to soften the blow: **Brothers, I entreat you, become as I am, for I also have become as you are** (**4:12**). That is, you took care of me. Now, I'm taking care of you. He reminds them that when he first came to them, he was suffering from a **bodily ailment**. Some have speculated it was malaria, an eye malady, or the cumulative effect of the beatings he suffered for the gospel. No one knows. What is known is that the Galatians **did not scorn or despise** him. They **received** him. Now, the roles are reversed. The Galatians are the ones in need of care. The Apostle is not there to scorn or despise. He is there to receive them: as an **angel of God, as Christ Jesus**. He asks them two important questions:

(1) **What has become of the blessing you felt?** Remember the good times?
(2) **Have I become your enemy by telling you the truth?** Would you rather me tell you what you *want* to hear or what you *need* to hear?

It would be odd for Paul to have become their enemy when—once upon a time—they would have **gouged out** their eyeballs for him. It is also odd, given that—once upon a time—they felt blessed by ministering to Paul's physical ailments. What changed?

Galatians 4:17–19. Don't Fall for Their Tactics. The Apostle sees through the nefarious strategy of these spiritual seducers: **They make much of you, but for no good purpose. They want to shut you out, that you may make much of them** (**4:17**). They make much of the Galatians because they want something in return: pleasure & prominence. They are as seducing as the adulterer who showers his unsuspecting prey with compliments and sweet whisperings; flirting and flattering her with endless gifts and surprises. It all seems so appealing at first. But there is (nearly always) a hidden motive. He who starts out so charming desires something sinister: pleasure, prominence, or both. It's all a self-serving game to the seducer.

The Apostle made much of them, true enough. But his purposes were pure. His gushings over them were for the good purpose of the gospel. The Apostle never asked anything in return. These seducers, on the other hand, follow age-old, self-promoting tactics. The

Apostle now lies **in the anguish of childbirth until Christ is formed** in the Galatians. This is another shadowy reference to his doubts concerning their salvation. Heartsick, the Apostle is trying—with passionate pleas—to awaken them to the tactics of these sly, spiritual seducers.

Galatians 4:20. Your Actions Are Inconsistent with the Gospel. Paul yearns for two things that are not possible at the moment: (1) that he **could be present** with them and (2) that he **could change** his **tone**. He concludes: **I am perplexed about you**. The Apostle was not perplexed by many things. He saw life as "black and white." This issue puzzled him, though. It caused him deep consternation. Those whom he had poured his life into ... who had cared for him when he was ailing ... who had received the gospel with joy ... were now in the process of rejecting the freedom he brought to them in the gospel. For what? To go back into slavery? To be coddled by seducers? It didn't make sense. The Galatians were acting in a manner inconsistent with the gospel they once believed.

Sermon Summary

If we follow the Apostle's intent (and we always should), this sermon is addressed to the person who has made a "profession of faith," but whose life is not presently matching that profession. It addresses several persons: (1) the person who may "be" saved, but is teetering toward another gospel; (2) the person who may "think" he's saved, but in reality, is not; or (3) the person who "is" truly saved, to whom this letter serves as a reminder of how easy it is to be seduced. It is entirely appropriate to preach from this text a sermon entitled, "**It's Time to Have the Tough Conversation**." I've had many of these conversations privately and seen many people come to faith in Christ. They are tough conversations because most people think they are saved. However, asking the tough questions can lead to true gospel conversion. Paul never shied away from being brutally honest about one's spiritual condition: He was concerned. It is too important to remain silent.

You will get mixed reactions from this sermon. I watched my grandmother have a tough conversation with a family member. She was concerned about his salvation. He was not living a life consistent with the gospel. She expressed her concern and asked if he were truly saved. He reacted angrily and chastised her for questioning his faith. At the same time, he was living in open sin. My grandmother since has passed away. But when she stood before God, she stood before him with a clear conscience that she tried all within her power to share the true gospel. We can say:

> *Some receive it happily; salvation soon is born.*
> *Some receive it angrily; the messenger is scorned.*
> *Some receive it neutrally; for those we truly mourn.*
> *However they receive it, though, we sound that gospel horn.*

Title: It's Time to Have the Tough Conversation

    I.   Here's What You Need to Hear (4:8-11)

    II.   What Changed? (4:12-16)

    III.   Don't Fall for Satan's Tactics (4:17-19)

    IV.   Your Actions Are Inconsistent with the Gospel (4:20)

As stated above, the dominant theme is the "heart-to-heart" nature of Paul's tone. The doctrine has been set. The arguments have been voiced. Now, he speaks to their hearts. His words (**afraid, anguish, perplexed**) show the personal nature of his tone.

GALATIANS 4:21–5:1
LOOK AT THE BIG PICTURE

After making an emotional heart-appeal, Paul can't resist returning to the OT for one last aerial view. He summarizes the OT by lifting-out two individuals who personify the Old and New Testaments: Hagar (Old) and Sarah (New). The Apostle speaks in general, sweeping terms here. Therefore, we shouldn't press the details too far. He states from the outset that he is **interpreting allegorically (Gal 4:24)**. The term **allegorically** occurs only here in the NT. We think of "allegory" as saying one thing on the surface but meaning something deeper underneath the words. That is not how the term was used in the 1st century. Without getting super-technical, J. K. Woollcombe's excellent etymological analysis proves the term meant "figurative language" when Paul used it.[35] Today, we liken it to a "metaphor." The Apostle, then, is asking his readers to look at these two women metaphorically as a demonstration of his point.

---

[35] K. J. Woollcombe, "The Biblical Origins and Patristic Development of Typology," in G. W. H. Lampe and K. J. Woollcombe, *Essays on Typology* (Naperville, IL: Alec R. Allenson, 1957), 50n1.

Galatians 4:21–27. Rejoice in Your Freedom!
The Apostle summarizes the OT teaching this way: You are either a child of the promise or a child of the flesh. Hagar represents children of the flesh. Sarah represents children of the promise. To back up a moment, God had promised Abraham that he would have a son (**Gen 15**). Sarah was unable to bear children (**Gen 16:1**). Therefore, she suggested that Abraham impregnate their Egyptian slave, Hagar, and he did (**Gen 16**). That consummation produced a child—not **born through promise**, but—**according to the flesh**, Ishmael.

Later, God opened Sarah's womb, and she bore the promised child, Isaac, whose progeny later would become Israel. The Apostle's metaphor runs this way: Hagar, the slave woman, represents the **flesh**, slavery to the old **covenant**, or **Mount Sinai** (the Apostle uses those terms synonymously). Metaphorically, she bears children under slavery to the law. By contrast, Sarah, the free woman, represents the faith-**promise**, freedom in the new **covenant**, or heavenly **Jerusalem** (the Apostle uses those terms synonymously). Metaphorically, she bears spiritual children of faith.

Therefore, Hagar represents **present Jerusalem**: that is, Jews enslaved by the law in the first century. Sarah represents the **Jerusalem above**: that is, spiritual Jerusalem (the church), the sum aggregate those set free from works-based slavery in every generation—from Adam until now.

The Apostle cites **Isaiah 54** to stamp his point with Scripture-authority. This passage likens Jerusalem to a barren widow, mourning at the city gates. Her husband (the people of Israel) has been taken away into captivity. God breaks through her mourning to say, "**Rejoice!**" God will make the children of the promise to be greater than the one who **has a husband**! In context, this means Hagar and her husband (i.e., the law) will spawn children. But Sarah's children of promise will outnumber Hagar's children of works. The Apostle, in effect, is suggesting: "You Galatian church members! You don't want to be a child of the flesh, do you? Yet, that is precisely the direction you are going." Luther's language may be archaic, but it is accurate nonetheless: "They ... bring forth many children, children that are bastards like themselves, children born to be put out of the house like Ishmael to perish forever."[36]

Galatians 4:28–5:1. Get Rid of Those Persecuting You! To trace out the metaphor, Paul petitions them to get rid of the fanatics. He skips to the end of the Sarah/Hagar feud in Genesis for his final point. Hagar's child (Ishmael) was found mocking Sarah's child (Isaac) (**Gen 21:9**). In response, Sarah demands that Abraham cast out the slave woman, which he does. Based on that historical context, Paul's metaphor continues along this track:

(1) You, Galatians, are **children of promise** (of Sarah).
(2) The fanatics are children **according to the flesh** (of Hagar).

---

[36] Luther, *Galatians*, 184.

(3) Flesh-children always have (and will) persecute Spirit-children (**Gal 4:29**).
(4) Therefore, **cast out the slave woman and her son** (**Gal 4:30**).

A part of me wishes the Apostle to have followed up with this: "Now, excommunicate the fanatics." He did not. He concludes with: **we are not children of the slave but of the free woman**. Nevertheless, when we consider the Apostle's wider body of work, we can safely conclude that the implication is to rid the church of the fanatics. Paul would not have put up with them in the church.

I included **5:1** in this section because the thought carries forward. Most commentaries do not. However, **5:2** is clean a break in which Paul changes direction (**Look**, he says—a clear shift). Therefore, **5:1** should be included as an exhortation: **stand firm** against false teaching (and bullies) in the church.

Sermon Summary

This sermon will address false teaching in the contemporary church. False teaching can be difficult to define. False teachers are slippery. Therefore, each expositor will need to bone-up on how to specifically define false teaching. In the present case, Paul had substantive evidence that these fanatics were "adding to" the gospel. After speaking to the Galatians' hearts, he summarizes the OT in terms of faith vs. law. I titled this sermon, **"Look at the Big Picture:"**

I.   **Christ Can Set You Free (4:21–27)**
II.   **Stand Up to Those Persecuting You (4:28–5:1)**

Sometimes, we get caught-up in superficial arguments and menial doctrinal quirks. Paul calls his readers to keep the plain thing as the main thing, and the main thing as the plain thing: Justification is by faith, not works. Anything that threatens that must be cast out.

GALATIANS 5:2–12
A LITTLE LEAVEN LEAVENS THE
WHOLE LUMP

The timeless principle in these two paragraphs is found in **Galatians 5:9: A little leaven leavens the whole lump**. The first paragraph (**5:2–6**) prefaces that principle by showing how a seemingly small doctrinal quirk can have major salvific consequences. The second paragraph (**5:7–12**) is an exhortation *not* to be manipulated by personable people with poisonous precepts.

Galatians 5:2–6. Don't Be Silly. The essence of works-righteousness is this: You must attempt to keep every point of the law (not merely some). **I testify to every man who accepts circumcision that he is obligated to keep the whole law** (**5:3**). You can't have it both ways. You can't "pick-'n'-choose." **If you accept circumcision**, the Apostle reasons, then you must also put to death those who violate the Sabbath day (**Num 15**); return any property you own in the Year of Jubilee (**Lev 25**); stone your child if he is rebellious (**Deut 21**); and a thousand other shibboleths. "Nonsense!" the Apostle declares, "Who is it that determines which laws we follow

(like **circumcision**) versus which ones we disregard
(like shaving our whiskers—**Lev 19:27**)?" The law is not a
buffet line in which we pick-'n'-choose items we like
while passing over items we don't like. No, the law is "all-
or-nothing."

Paul is not condemning the law. He is condemning those who would be justified by it. They are inconsistent. Worse: **You are severed from Christ, you who
would be justified by the law; you have fallen away
from grace (5:4)**. To be severed from Christ is to be "al-
ienated from" him.[37] This statement is absolute: justification is either "all of Christ" or "none of Christ." There is
no in-between; no hybrid approach; no gray area. The
Apostle declares it definitively: Those who seek justification by law **have fallen away from grace**. Some transla-
tions render it "**you are fallen**" (KJV) or "**you have
fallen**" (NAS, NKJV). The Greek word (ἐξεπέσατε) can
mean either "fallen" or "fallen away."[38] Walt Kaiser probably is correct to suggest it is a falling away from the "*gospel system of salvation in Christ,*"[39] meaning the doctrines
of grace (or, the *ordo salutis*, as defined above). Luther likens it to falling from a ship into the sea. He adds:

> To fall from grace means to lose the atonement,
> the forgiveness of sins, the righteousness, liberty,

---

[37] Moo, *Galatians*, 326.

[38] *BDAG*, 307-08.

[39] Walter C. Kaiser, Jr., *Toward an Exegetical Theology: Biblical
Exegesis for Teaching and Preaching* (Grand Rapids: Baker Book House,
1981), 85, emphasis original.

and life which Jesus has merited for us by His death and resurrection. To lose the grace of God means to gain the wrath and judgment of God, death, the bondage of the devil, and everlasting condemnation.[40]

The Apostle is pressing them with this point: To seek to be justified by the law must not be taken lightly. It's not merely a debate or a difference of opinion. For Paul, it was the difference between standing before God as righteous or standing before God condemned. Of course, everyone knows that has eternal ramifications as well.

An interesting grammatical shift occurs here. Whereas he has been speaking of *you*—i.e., *you* are severed from Christ; *you* have fallen—he now shifts to *we* in **5:5. For through the Spirit, by faith, *we* ourselves eagerly wait for the hope of righteousness**. Notice, the Apostle invokes the work of the Spirit here—clearly delineating "us" (Spirit-children) from "them" (flesh-children). Indeed, faith itself is a gift given to us through the Spirit. The Apostle later states in another letter, **For by grace you have been saved through faith. And this is not your own doing; it is the gift of God** (Eph 2:8). Thank the Lord the Spirit gifts faith to us! For as with all else, if it were dependent upon us, we would fail miserably! Such Spirit-wrought faith gives us hope of righteousness. It is important to note that hope is not wishful thinking. Rather, it is future certainty not yet realized. The Apostle aptly introduces the Spirit's work in

---

[40] Martin Luther, *Galatians*, 169-70

regeneration here and will expand upon his work in sanctification shortly.

The larger point to which the Apostle has his bow aimed: Stop entertaining their nonsense! You can't pick-'n'-choose which OT laws you prefer. You either live by them all and be judged by them all ... or else simply trust—by faith—that Christ lived by them all for you and was judged by them all in your place. Those are the only two options.

Galatians 5:7–12. Don't Be Manipulated by Malcontents. The key phrase here is the proverbial statement, **A little leaven leavens the whole lump**. Leaven, in ancient times, was what we might call "yeast" today. It was added to dough in small amounts to make it rise. It made bread softer and tastier, as well as more filling. A little would permeate the whole. In Scripture, **leaven** can be used to portray good things or bad things. Here, it characterizes the evil teachings the fanatics were spewing. A similar, more modern-day proverb might be, "They poisoned the well." Another example is rat poison. Rat poison is made up of less than 1% poison. The other 99% is inert (inactive) ingredients. The 1% is what kills.

The Apostle pronounces judgment on the spiritual rats (**5:10**). In **5:11**, he says something which is confusing at first glance, **But if I, brothers, still preach circumcision, why am I still being persecuted?** But Paul is not preaching circumcision! What is going on here? Well, Paul once *did* preach circumcision—before he was converted. Apparently, the fanatics were playing loose with the facts. They seem to have been asserting that their teachings and Paul's were consistent. "Never!" Paul cries. If that were the case, **the offense of the cross has been removed**. That is, the cross becomes meaningless. May it never be!

Paul's final wish is gory: If the fanatics are so obsessed with cutting other men's foreskins, then he wishes they would castrate (**emasculate**) themselves (**5:12**)!

Sermon Summary

These two paragraphs deserve treatment as one sermon. A title could be simply "**A Little Leaven Leavens the Whole Lump**." These two paragraphs are Paul's final appeal before launching into practical applications that flow out of justification by faith alone. Each paragraph deserves its own point:

I.   **Don't Be Silly (5:2–6)**
II.   **Don't Be Manipulated (5:7–12)**

The point to bring out is that we must be very careful when handling doctrine. A little poison mixed with a lot of good is still poisonous.

GALATIANS 5:13–15
LIBERTY VERSUS LICENTIOUSNESS

The grammar here clearly marks this section as the closing bell. All arguments have been made. All that is left now is to show how the gospel is relevant in real life. This section deals with Christian liberties. Christian liberty is a dicey topic—then and now—because it seems so subjective. If we are free from the law, then what are we free to do or not do? Man has a tendency to go to from one extreme or the other: total law-keeping or total licentiousness. Rare is the person who uses his/her freedom with God-honoring responsibility. The prisoner who is suddenly released from prison has a tendency to gorge himself with food. Why? Because, in prison, he was bound by the law as to mealtimes and food portions. With all rules removed, he is free to eat all he wants whenever he wants. Gorging himself is not healthy. The Apostle provides a principled response to Christian freedom. He gets more specific later, but the core concept is this: Are your actions self-serving or serving others?

Galatians 5:13a. You Were Called to Freedom.
We must remember three things here. First, the word *for*

at the beginning of the verse is critical. It's as if the Apostle says, "Based on my previous point, I now will make a conclusion. My previous point was this: Christ satisfied the law's demands for you. Based on this truth, I declare that '**You were called to freedom, brothers**.'" Remember, the Apostle knew many of these people.

The phrase **you were called** is the second concept to remember. In Greek, it is a passive voice, meaning that the subject (**you**) is acted upon. You didn't do anything. God did. This refers to God's effectual call. **God called you to freedom**.

The third concept is the word *freedom*. We have certain freedoms but not total freedom. For instance, we can't yell "Fire!" in a crowded theatre. We live in a free country, but we don't have the freedom to steal another person's vehicle, intellectual property, wife, etc. You see, freedom is not a license to do whatever we desire. Rather, freedom—in this context—is the liberation from slavery to the law's demands and penalties—as well as from the guilt and condemnation that come with it. Yet, we must be careful to point out that it is not an independent self-governance to do as we wish without repercussion.

Galatians 5:13b. Do Not Abuse Your Freedom.
It should be obvious now that freedom carries with it a certain measure of responsibility: **Do not use your freedom as an opportunity for the flesh** (5:13). One thing on which the Apostle and his opponents agree: All men inherit a nature inclined toward sin. Come, watch my children scheme and provoke and even strike one another, and you will agree. I never taught them those

things. They instinctively perform those acts because they inherited them from their father. Surely, the Apostle's opponents were leveling this charge, "If you are free from the law (as Paul asserts), then there is nothing left to restrain sin! This cannot be! Every man would do that which was right in his own eyes!" Fanatics—yes. But they raise a valid objection.

Paul responds: Do not use your freedom as an opportunity for the flesh. The word *flesh* refers to pleasures (lusts) of the mind, will, or body. He later specifies several of them: **sexual immorality, jealousy, dissensions, fits of anger**, etc. All can be reduced to this: self-serving acts. The Apostle valiantly proclaims, "You are free from the law—yes! But your freedom carries a responsibility to represent Christ, not your own self-interests! Genuine Christians live according to the former and opposed to the latter."

Galatians 5:13c–15. Serve One Another. Here we find the heart of the guiding principle related to Christian liberty: **Through love, serve one another**. Self-serving versus serving others. The Greek word underlying "**serve**" is *douleuete* (which is related to the Greek word for *slave*). Literally, it reads, "act as a slave" to one another in love.[41] If Christians hold this guiding principle, then the law takes a backseat to the higher virtue it represents: **love** rooted in the ground (or, bottom) of the heart.

---

[41] Moo, *Galatians*, 345.

Every point of the law is designed either to *reveal* man's lack of love or to *restrain* man's lack of love. This is how the Apostle summarizes it: **The whole law is fulfilled in one word: "You shall love your neighbor as yourself."** He speaks generally, of course; but his point is well taken. If every man "loved his neighbor as himself," then the law—for most intents and purposes—is unnecessary.

The Apostle digs further: If you **bite one another**, you are self-serving rather than serving others. If you **devour one another**, the same thing holds true. Animals act this way in fending only for themselves. Moo states, "The comparison describes mad beasts fighting each other so ferociously that they end up killing each other."[42] If your focus is on "self" rather than "others," no one wins. You have only fed your beastly ego.

Sermon Summary

This sermon will deal with Christian liberty. We are free from the law's demands and penalty. However, we must use our new freedom responsibly. Paul's audience asked questions such as, "Can I eat meat sacrificed to idols? Can I eat meat that is unclean (bacon)?" Our audiences ask questions like, "Can a Christian drink alcohol? Must a Christian tithe? Can I work or Sunday? Can I get a tattoo? Can I attend a gay wedding?" Such questions will change as cultures change. Paul answers them, not

---

[42] Moo, *Galatians*, 349.

with specifics (he knew specifics would change with time), but with timeless principles. The title of this sermon might be, **"Freedom Versus Free-for-all."** These points capture the gist of the Apostle's message:

> I.   **You Have Been Set Free! (5:13a)**
> II.   **Do Not Abuse Your Freedom! (5:13b)**
> III.   **Serve One Another (5:13c–15)**

In summary, several abstracted principles will need to be set forth.

> (1) *When Scripture speaks clearly, so must we.* When Scripture says, **And do not get drunk with wine, for that is debauchery, but be filled with the Spirit (Eph 5:18)**, then we can say confidently that drunkenness is a sin. Can a Christian drink? Perhaps. Perhaps not, depending on the situation. But we can clearly say that a Christian is not to get drunk. What does it mean to get drunk: the third beer or the fourth? The fourteenth sip or the fifteenth? This is where Christian liberty is difficult to pin-down. In such cases, it probably is best to abide by principle #2 (below).
>
> (2) *When it causes your brother to stumble, consider refraining.* The Apostle *did not* exercise his Christian freedom when he circumcised Timothy in **Acts 16**. He could have refused to have Timothy circumcised, but he refrained from exercising that refusal. He did not want to

offend Jewish believers. By contrast, the Apostle did exercise his Christian freedom when he refused to circumcise Titus in **Galatians 2:3**. He did so because nefarious fanatics were demanding it. Paul expounds in another place (**1 Cor 8**) that, while we have the freedom to eat meats sacrificed to idols, we must count other believers more significant than ourselves. If it offends another believer, sometimes it is best to refrain. Use sound judgment, of course. You cannot live your life solely based on what others "might" perceive. Yet often, if we surrender some of our rights, we strengthen another brother and make the kingdom stronger.

(3) *Better safe than sorry.* As a general principle: If you err, err on the conservative side of an issue. You may have the freedom to do many things. However, if a question arises, often it is best to err on the conservative side rather than the liberal side of an issue. Generally speaking, I believe God will understand when you stand before him if you were loving your neighbor more than yourself. If you err on the side of liberality because it feeds your fleshly appetites or to make a point to weaker brothers—even if you might be able to justify your Christian freedom to do so—then you may find yourself blushing at his throne. It goes back to motive: Are you serving self or others?

Certainly, there are other principles to consider. These shall suffice for now.

GALATIANS 5:16–26
HOLY WAR

There is a holy war going on within every believer. Our flesh always will incline us toward Christian freedom because the flesh is concerned with one person: self. The Spirit will balance us because the Spirit is concerned with one principle: exalting the Son of God through heartfelt truth. That is, truth mixed with the right emotion, attitude, motive, and agenda. Indeed, we may have the Christian freedom to "do" some things, but the Spirit helps us surrender our rights when our emotions, attitudes, motives, or agendas may not be pure. Surrendering our rights is not easy. In fact, it is a continual inner war of the Spirit versus flesh.

Galatians 5:16–18. Spirit Versus Flesh. Those who have the Spirit ultimately *will* use their newfound freedom responsibly: **But I say, walk by the Spirit, and you will not gratify the desires of the flesh** (**5:16**). To walk by the Spirit means to live a life characterized by Spirit-qualities (enumerated in **5:22–23**). The Apostle then explains the holy war inside the believer's heart (**5:17**). The flesh rages against the Spirit. The Spirit rages

against the flesh. Each has declared war on the other. Before you had the Spirit, no such war existed. You lived—
quite ignorantly—in the passions of your flesh, carrying
out the desires of your body and mind (**Eph 2:3**). When
you received the Spirit, however, part of his task is to
keep you from doing the things you want to do (5:17).
This is an age-old battle. Paul concludes, noting: If you
follow the Spirit's lead, then the law is unnecessary because you will be living according to an even higher
standard than the law was able to set.

Galatians 5:19–21. Fleshly Works Lead to Hell.
Those who **walk** (live a life characterized) according to
the **flesh**, says the Apostle, **will not inherit the kingdom of God (5:21)**. He proceeds to offer a shortlist of
fleshly works. We will look at each in turn, but we must
be careful here not to hastily condemn. The Apostle is not
suggesting that an occasional fleshly work or isolated
fleshly works condemn to hell. Otherwise, no one would
inherit the kingdom of God. At one time or another, all
Spirit-children have been guilty of one or more fleshly
works—even after conversion. The language is clear: He
is referring to a life in which such works become a pat-
tern. Moo discusses them in detail.[43]

| (1) | **Sexual immorality**: | general term referring to sexual sins of any kind |
| (2) | **Impurity**: | sexual misbehavior, as Paul uses the term elsewhere |

[43] Moo, *Galatians*, 359–62.

(3) **Sensuality**:   wild life or being a "party animal"

(4) **Idolatry**:   anything that competes with God for our affections

(5) **Sorcery**:   *pharmakeia* – use of drugs in general or in magical practices, or to exert undue influence over another (as in **Rev 18:23**)

(6) **Enmity**:   human-against-human hatred

(7) **Strife**:   discord or quarreling

(8) **Jealousy**:   arousal of fear, rage, humiliation, or abandonment due to actions from a third party

(9) **Fits of anger**:   outbursts of rage

(10) **Rivalries**:   expressions of selfish ambition

(11) **Dissensions**:   actions of an organized party of mal contents

(12) **Divisions**:   actions upsetting people with intent to disrupt

(13) **Envy**:   an emotion evoked when a person lacks an other's superior qualities, achievement, or possessions

(14) **Drunkenness**:   inebriation

(15) **Orgies**:   feasts or celebrations often involving alcohol and/or sexual liberties

With the exceptions of sexual immorality, drunkenness, and orgies, I have seen many of these works in church meetings and have often wondered if those exceptions weren't taking place somewhere else as well!

Galatians 5:22–24. True Believers Will Bear True Fruit. Christ would have us bear the **fruit of** his **Spirit** instead. The **fruit of the Spirit** stands in stark

contrast to the **works of the flesh**. Again, Moo provides
details:[44]

(1)	**Love**:	*agape* – self-sacrificial love, which complements the focus on serving others rather than self-interest
(2)	**Joy**:	settled disposition arising from acceptance by God
(3)	**Peace**:	harmonious and loving relationship (with God and men)
(4)	**Patience**:	the enduring of difficult circumstances or people without negativity
(5)	**Kindness**:	gracious response to rebellious creatures
(6)	**Goodness**:	generosity toward others
(7)	**Faithfulness**:	someone in whom complete confidence can be placed
(8)	**Gentleness**:	not being overly impressed with one's self-importance
(9)	**Self-control**:	regulation of one's emotions, attitude, and behavior in the light of temptations or impulses

The feature that distinguishes the lists is easily observed.
The works of the flesh are self-serving. The fruit of the
Spirit is "otherly." That is why **against such things
there is no law (5:23)**. This Spirit-led realm supersedes
even the lofty standard the law signified. To walk in the
fruit of the Spirit is the very picture of what the entirety
of the law represents. **Galatians 5:24: And those who**

---

[44] Moo, *Galatians*, 365–67.

belong to Jesus Christ have crucified the flesh with its passions and desires. To crucify does not mean to destroy totally. Rather, it means the flesh's power is broken.[45] Only the children **led by the Spirit (5:18)** can live victoriously over the flesh.

Galatians 5:25–26. If You Talk the Talk, You Must Walk the Walk. The Apostle counsels: **If we live by the Spirit, let us also keep in step with the Spirit (5:25)**. His reasoning is sound. If you are **led by the Spirit (5:18)**, you will live by the Spirit. It won't do to claim Spirit-empowerment while, at the same time, living in a fleshly manner. Inherited sin continually pulls at us (and sometimes wins). However, these will be isolated instances and will decrease over time. We never will reach perfection; that is not possible. Yet, the Spirit will help us sin less and hate sin all the more. If we claim we have the Spirit, let us also walk like we have him.

Paul highlights three qualities representative of others that are inconsistent with Spirit-led lives when he says **Let us not become conceited, provoking one another, envying one another**. The word Paul uses for *conceit* combines two Greek words meaning *empty* and *praise*. It refers to the person who might think he has a right to glory and acclaim when he does not. Such a one is full of "empty praise."[46] *Provoking one another* refers to aggressively challenging another or imposing one's will

---

[45] Moo, *Galatians*, 368.
[46] Moo, *Galatians*, 373.

on another.[47] *Envying one another* (Paul uses a verb related to the noun found in **5:21**) refers to that dark emotion arising when one lacks another's superior achievements, qualities, or possessions. It often leads to other passions of the flesh such as rage, bitterness, suspicion, etc., that—when acted upon—can result in violence or death.

Sermon Summary

This sermon deals with the inner struggle of every believer: **The Holy War**. First, the Apostle speaks of the participants in the war: flesh vs. Spirit. Second, he speaks of the weaponry of the flesh. Third, he speaks of the weaponry of the Spirit. Last, he makes a concluding point: You cannot serve in both armies.

I.   **Your Spirit Versus Your Flesh (5:16-18)**
II.   **Your Fleshly Works Lead to Hell (5:19-21)**
III. **Spirit-Fruit Leads to Bliss (5:22-24)**
IV.   **If You Talk the Talk, Then Walk the Walk (5:25-26)**

Drawing from the previous section, this is truly about self-service versus serving others. Tying this section back to **5:13: Serve one another** (rather than yourself) will help connect the Apostle's flow of thought.

---

[47] Moo, *Galatians*, 373.

GALATIANS 6:1–10
MARKS OF JUSTIFICATION

The Apostle began in **Galatians 5:13** explaining how **Spirit**-people are to use their freedom from the law responsibly. He moves from the internal qualities the **Spirit** brings (**love, joy, peace,** etc.) to some external marks of those who have been justified by faith: (1) reach out to fallen Christians and (2) take good care of gospel teachers.

Galatians 6:1–5. Take Care of the Fallen (Spiritually). The imperative is, **Bear one another's burdens** (**6:2**). This is a general statement (we should be sensitive to all the needs/struggles of others). But it is given in a specific context, one regarding someone **caught in transgression**. Often, our knee-jerk reaction is to pile upon the one who has fallen to sin. We shake our heads, wag our fingers, and butcher his reputation. It shouldn't be so. We should run *to* him rather than *from* him. The text addresses **you who are spiritual**, a single word in Greek which refers to Spirit-children. Those who are led by the Spirit and live by the Spirit should also lift-up others by the Spirit. Too often we are quick to reprehend others like Pharisees did rather than **restore** others like Jesus did. The term "**restore**" is a present-tense verb indicating an ongoing process.[48] It takes care, compassion, and constancy. It is to be done in a **spirit of gentleness** (Paul uses the same word as he does in discussing the **fruit of the Spirit** in **Gal 5:23**) as opposed to harshness. There is a mild warning here (**6:1b**) not to become entangled in the **transgression** of the one who has fallen or the web his transgression might have spun.

It is in this restorative spirit that we are to **bear one another's burdens**. Doing so fulfills the **law of Christ**. The law of Christ is that higher spiritual law—from the ground of the heart—which the tablets of Moses represent. You can follow the Mosaic law outwardly while despising it inwardly: That is to say, you can tithe with your hands while hating it in your heart. The law of Christ is tithing with your hands from an overflowing desire to do so in your heart. The law of Christ leaves no room for pride (**6:3**). We must **test** our inner motives rather than compare ourselves with our **neighbor**. The depraved heart always will find a neighbor who is inferior by which to compare itself. The comparison must be to Christ. In the end, each of us must give an account to him, not a neighbor we cherry-picked. As the Apostle phrases it, **each will have to bear his own load**.

Galatians 6:6–10. Take Care of Your Teachers (Materially). As a pastor, I hesitate to speak about my own salary. Someone always will rise up and say in his

---

[48] Moo, *Galatians*, 375.

heart, "He's lobbying for more money." Yet, neither can we ignore this scriptural admonition. Martin Luther: "I have often wondered why all the apostles reiterated this request with such embarrassing frequency."[49] It is sad how God's men are treated today. The Scripture mandate is clear: **One who is taught the word must share all good things with the one who teaches (6:6)**. We have a biblical obligation to support, materially, our gospel teachers. **All good things** must not be limited to money. It also includes health, safety, encouragement, and general well-being. If the gospel teacher has the immense pressures of being doubly accountable to God and constantly hounded by spiritual attack, why do many churches pile-on the added pressures of making him suffer in other (earthly) areas? We should be overly generous, not overly stingy.

The Apostle follows this convicting line with an axiom **(6:7–8)**: You reap what you sow. Two points are obvious: (1) If you sow good things (spiritual), you reap good things. (2) If you sow bad things (fleshly), you reap bad things. Paul also makes two implicit points: (1) You always reap *more* than you sow. (2) You always reap *after* you sow. The principle is true generally, but here is given in the context of supporting your teachers. If you take care of them, they will take care of you. Why not invest in teachers? In doing so, you benefit as well.

Galatians 6:9–10 encourages us to do **good things** while we have time. Knowing there are more good things to do than can be done, the Apostle

---

[49] Luther, *Galatians*, 237.

prioritizes our efforts: We must look first to **the house-hold of faith** and, second, to those outside the kingdom of God. Common sense, naturally, should prevail when resources might be limited and when taking the urgency of the circumstance into consideration.

Sermon Summary

The Apostle's reasoning has run along these lines: (1) Justification is by faith (not works). (2) Justification by faith frees us from the law. (3) We must use that freedom responsibly. (4) The Spirit balances our natural inclination to abuse our freedom. (5) Spirit-children will be marked by a concern for others, especially those who teach them.

This sermon will expound the last of these five truths. The title will be something like, "**Marks of Spirit-Children**." The two paragraphs reflect two main points:

I.   **Take Care of the Fallen (Spiritually) (6:1-5)**
II.   **Take Care of Your Teachers (Materially) (6:6-10)**

It will be important to re-trace Paul's reasoning (as I did above) for the less-studied listeners. Justification by faith spawns godly behavior from a Spirit-filled heart, behavior such as the two marks listed here. These two are not exhaustive (Paul could have listed many), but representative. Likely, the Galatians were weak in these two areas, as are many churches today. Scripture confronts and corrects such deficiencies, and we would do well to heed Scripture's counsel.

GALATIANS 6:11–18
LOOK AT A PERSON'S
UNDERLYING MOTIVES

Now, the Apostle shuts-down his letter. He closes by striking at motive. For those still confused as to who to believe, the Apostle perceptively warns, "Look at their underlying motives: *They* seek the praise of men (**6:12a**). *They* seek the easy life (**6:12b**). *They* act hypocritically (**6:13a**). And *they* seek feathers in the cap (**6:13b**). *My* motive is single: the cross."

Galatians 6:11-13. Look at Their Motives. The Apostle does something unusual here. Typically, he dictated his letters to an assistant. Here, he writes personally. This adds another layer of urgency to his tone. This surprise offers us a hint that what comes next is worthy of attention. Indeed, it is. The Apostle deals a parting blow to the motives of these irrational animals.

They seek the praises of men. **They want to make a good showing in the flesh**. They desire popularity, pats on the back, and clapping of hands. They want to impress men so that men will be impressed by them. Many do the same today. They prefer the parts of Scripture that tickle men's ears. They avoid difficult doctrines or any mention of sin, judgment, wrath, or hellfire. Paul did not come in that spirit. He sought the praise of God (not men) by preaching the whole counsel: redemption and damnation; damnation and redemption.

They seek ease of life. They do not want to **be persecuted by the cross of Christ**, so they avoid (or gloss over) the cross. They divert attention to **circumcision** and scrupulous observations of **days and months and seasons and years**. "But let us stay at an arms-length distance from the cross," they imply, "It strikes a nerve in men. It drives many men away. It confronts the will of the flesh and causes men to kick against the pricks." They do the same in our day. "Speak of any doctrine," they champion, "but steer clear of the cross. It is a bloody, messy thing that divides rather than unites. Uplift, encourage, motivate, coach 'em up—Ah, yes! That will keep them coming back." Such ne'er-do-wells scrunch-up their noses at the cross. Not so with the Apostle. The cross was the centerpiece of his message.

They live in a state of hypocrisy. They adjure you to follow this or that rule. We have covered this already (see **Galatians 5:2-6**). Who chooses which rules to follow? They assert that you break the law by not cutting the flesh of your foreskins. Do they not break the law by failing to offer tithes of the firstfruits? Why do they uphold the former but reject the latter? The Apostle may have been headstrong, short-tempered (at times), or even disagreeable at times (with John Mark, for instance), but he did not live in a state of hypocrisy.

They seek feathers in the cap. Like Indians who add a feather to their headdress after stalking and overpowering their prey, these hunters seek converts to add to their trumped-up resumes. It is all too common today. When I encounter other teachers or preachers, the question asked most often is this: "How many are you running in Sunday School? How many are you running in worship?" Rare is the day when they ask, "How healthy is your church? How faithful is your church to Scripture? Are your members moving to deeper levels of discipleship?" No, it's a numbers game today. "How much flesh can you accumulate?" That was the gold standard then and is now, it seems. Such busybodies **boast in your flesh**. The Apostle was more concerned with the state of their souls and their progression in sanctification.

Galatians 6:14–15. Look at My Motive. Paul says, **But far be it from me to boast except in the cross of our Lord Jesus Christ, by which the world has been crucified to me, and I to the world (6:14)**. He had appealed on this basis once before (see **Gal 4:12–20**). "I told you once before," pleads the Apostle, "I came with no false motive, but because of a bodily ailment. So I say again, 'I came to you not to puff up myself, my ministry, or my numbers. I came to boast in the cross.'" Luther clarifies, "By the Cross of Christ is not to be understood here the two pieces of wood to which He was nailed, but all the afflictions of the believers whose sufferings are Christ's sufferings."[50] It includes both the identification with

---

[50] Luther, *Galatians*, 244.

Christ as our substitute on the cross *and* the worldly sufferings that come with that identification. My identification with the cross-event, then, causes me to condemn—
crucify—the world-system (the lust of the flesh, the lust
of the eyes, and the pride of life). Vice-versa, the world-
system condemns—crucifies—me as foolish, weak—an
ignorant simpleton.

"No matter!" heralds the Apostle, "God will have
the last laugh." God chose that which was weak in the
world to shame the strong so that no man may boast. **Neither circumcision nor uncircumcision matter**. What
matters is the heart: the **new creation**. Timothy George
describes the new creation (i.e., new birth) brilliantly:

> The new creation, then, involves the whole pro-
> cess of conversion: the regenerating work of the
> Holy Spirit leading to repentance and faith, the
> daily process of mortification and vivification,
> continual growth in holiness.... The new creation
> implies a new nature with a new system of de-
> sires, affections, and habits, all wrought through
> the supernatural ministry of the Holy Spirit.... No
> spiritual gymnastics, no twelve-step program on
> the deeper life, no quick-fix "How-to-Be-a-Bet-
> ter-Christian" seminar can produce this kind of
> transformation.... No one is made right with God
> on the basis of external ceremonies or human ef-
> forts of any kind but only through the unilateral
> action of God in the cross and resurrection of Je-
> sus Christ.... Put otherwise, justification by faith

is not a legal fiction but a living reality that manifests itself in the new creation.[51]

Far from a ritualistic system of rule-keeping, the new creation spawns a Christ-honoring life from the ground of the heart. It requires heart surgery. That is, it involves an operation of the Spirit whereby he removes the heart of stone and replaces it with the heart of Christ. The Apostle knew from experience: You cannot legislate morality. You must have a heart transformation.

Galatians 6:16–18. Closing Remarks. The Apostle has said everything that can be said. He bids us adieu with a prayer-wish of **peace**, **mercy**, and **grace**. **Peace** is the absence of war. It refers to the calm that ensues when God removed his wrath from us and placed it upon his Son on the cross. **Mercy** means you "don't" get what you "do" deserve. We deserve hell, but we don't get it. **Grace** (**6:18**) means you "do" get what you "don't" deserve. We deserve nothing for our sin-labors, but we receive heaven's reward. It is unmerited, undeserved; but it is ours. He adds this heavenly prayer-wish upon the **Israel of God**. He made clear in **3:7** that this phrase refers to all who are justified by faith—whether Jew or Gentile.

The Apostle has done all he can do. He taught them in person. He prayed for them with passion. He wrote to them with clarity. With a certain sense of exasperation, he concludes: **From now on let no one cause me trouble, for I bear on my body the marks of Jesus**.

---

[51] George, *Galatians*, 438–39.

"I have physical pain from my sufferings for Christ," Paul laments, "Add to that the mental and emotional anguish over your perplexing ways.... I am spent. I have done all I can do."

Sermon Summary

This sermon centers on the motive of ministry. Compare/contrast false motives from pure ones. In doing so, false teachers will be exposed. Pure ministers will be exonerated. A good title might be, **Look at a Person's Underlying Motive**:

    I.   **Look at Their Motives (6:11-13)**
    II.   **Look at My Motives (6:14-15)**
    III.   **Final Thoughts (6:16-18)**

Follow Paul's emphasis. Focus on Points 1 and 2. Point 3 should be brief.

BIBLIOGRAPHY

Arndt, William, Frederick W. Danker, Walter Bauer, and
 F. Wilbur Gingrich. *A Greek-English Lexicon of the
 New Testament and Other Early Christian Litera-
 ture.* Chicago: University of Chicago Press, 2000.

Bumgardner, Chuck. "Paul in Arabia." Accessible online:
 https://cbumgardner.word-
 press.com/2011/11/18/paul-in-ara/. November
 11, 2011. Accessed April 9, 2022.

Calvin, John. *Commentaries on the Epistle of Paul the Apostle to the Romans.* Translated by John Owen. Edinburgh: Calvin Translation Society, 1849.

Calvin, John. *The Epistles of Paul the Apostle to the Galatians, Ephesians, Philippians and Colossians.* Translated by T. H. L. Parker. Calvin's Commentaries.
 Grand Rapids: Eerdmans, 1965.

George, Timothy. *Galatians.* New American Commentary 30. Nashville: Broadman & Holman, 1994.

Grudem, Wayne, ed. *The ESV Study Bible*. Wheaton, IL: Crossway, 2008.

Kaiser, Jr., Walter C. *Toward an Exegetical Theology: Biblical Exegesis for Preaching and Teaching.* Grand Rapids: Baker Book House, 1981.

Luther, Martin. *Commentary on the Epistle to the Galatians*. Translated by Theodore Graebner. Grand Rapids: Zondervan, 1949.

MacArthur, John. *The MacArthur Study Bible*. Nashville: Thomas Nelson, 2006.

Moo, Douglas J. *Galatians*. Baker Exegetical Commentary on the New Testament. Grand Rapids: Zondervan, 2013.

Tyndale, William. *The Parable of the Wicked Mammon*, 1527 (accessible online).

Tyndale, William. *Tyndale's New Testament*. New Haven and London: Yale University Press, 1989.

Woollcombe, K. J. "The Biblical Origins and Patristic Development of Typology." Pages 39–75 in G. W. H. Lampe and K. J. Woollcombe. *Essays on Typology*. Naperville, IL: Alec R. Allenson, 1957.